The Conflict Resolution Library™

Dealing with Hurt Feelings

• Lisa K. Adams •

The Rosen Publishing Group's
PowerKids Press
New York

Published in 1997 by The Rosen Publishing Group, Inc.
29 East 21st Street, New York, NY 10010

First Edition

Book Design: Erin McKenna

Photo Illustrations: Cover and all photo illustrations by Carrie Ann Grippo.

Adams, Lisa K.
    Dealing with hurt feelings/ by Lisa K. Adams.
       p.   cm. — (The conflict resolution library)
    Includes index.
    Summary: Discusses what to do when your feelings get hurt or when you hurt someone else's feelings.
    ISBN 0-8239-5075-1
    1. Emotions in children—Juvenile literature. 2. Expression in children—Juvenile literature. [1. Emotions.
    2. Behavior.] I. Title. II. Series.
    BF723.E6A32 1997
    155.4'124—dc21

                                       97-4150
                                         CIP
                                         AC

Manufactured in the United States of America

Contents

Danny and Joe

Danny called Joe a mean name at school. Joe's feelings were hurt. He was also angry. He called Danny a name back.

Both boys started yelling terrible things at each other. They made each other so upset, they both began to cry. Then they got in trouble with the teacher for **arguing** (AR-gyoo-ing).

Did Danny and Joe feel better after they hurt each other's feelings? No. They felt worse.

◀ Arguing won't solve the problem between you and your friend.

When Do Feelings Get Hurt?

There are a lot of ways feelings can get hurt. Has anyone ever called you a mean name? Did one of your friends at school have a party and not invite you?

When someone's feelings get hurt, they feel sad and **lonely** (LOHN-lee). Sometimes they feel a little angry. Everyone's feelings get hurt sometimes. This book will help you know what to do when your feelings are hurt or when you hurt someone else's feelings.

A person's feelings can be hurt if they are left out of something that others are doing.

Hurting Back Doesn't Help

When someone hurts your feelings, you may get angry and want to do the same thing back to that person. But that doesn't **solve** (SOLV) the problem.

Hurting people's feelings just because they have hurt yours only makes things worse. Everyone becomes angry and everyone's feelings stay hurt.

◀ Being angry at someone can make you feel bad, too.

What Should You Do?

When your feelings get hurt, don't hold the hurt feelings inside. The best thing to do is to get your feelings out by talking to a friend, parent, or teacher. Tell that person how you feel about what happened.

You will start to feel better as soon as you start talking about it. Just knowing someone cares about how you feel will help make those hurt feelings go away.

Talk about what happened with someone you trust. ▶

Talk It Out

Now you have to decide if you want to talk to the person who hurt your feelings. If it is someone you care about, it is best to talk to him.

Chances are he isn't feeling very good about what happened either. Let him know that he hurt your feelings. Give him a chance to explain what he did and why he did it. Once you talk it out, both of you will feel better.

◀ Listening to someone is just as important as talking about how you feel.

Joanna and Nancy

One day, Joanna fell off her bike and hurt herself. Instead of helping her, Joanna's sister, Nancy, laughed and made fun of her. Joanna's feelings were hurt.

Nancy felt bad about hurting her sister's feelings. She knew that it had been mean to laugh at Joanna. So Nancy **apologized** (uh-POL-uh-jyzd) and asked Joanna if she was okay. The sisters made up and they both felt much better.

How would you feel if someone made fun of you? ▶

When You Feel Mean

Has there ever been a time when you have hurt someone else's feelings? Maybe you called someone a name at school or you told your little brother or sister to go away when he or she wanted to play with you.

We have all been mean to someone at one time or another. Sometimes we are **moody** (MOO-dee) and we don't feel like being nice. But that doesn't mean it is okay to hurt someone's feelings.

◀ It's never okay to hurt someone's feelings.

When Feelings Are Hurt

The first thing to do when you've hurt someone's feelings is to think about why you did it. Were you angry at the person? Were you just in a bad mood? Thinking about it will help you understand why you were mean. Once you understand this, you can fix the **situation** (sit-choo-AY-shun).

Understanding why you hurt someone's feelings is the first step towards making things better. ▶

Apologize

Once you've thought about why you have hurt someone's feelings, the next step is to talk to that person. Explain why you did what you did. Then the person can understand how you feel.

Next you should apologize. Tell the person that you are sorry for what you did. That will make him or her feel a lot better. Even though apologizing can be hard, you will feel better too.

◀ Apologizing can be hard, but it will make both of you feel better.

Everyone Has Bad Days

Everyone has good days and bad days. Sometimes we feel mean on our bad days. We may hurt someone else's feelings. One of our friends may hurt our feelings too.

The next time you hurt someone's feelings, think about why you did it. Think about how you would feel if that person had hurt your feelings. Then apologize and talk about what happened. You both will feel better and you will stay friends.

Glossary

apologize (uh-POL-uh-jyz) To say you are sorry
    for something you did or said.

arguing (AR-gyoo-ing) When two people talk
    about something on which they disagree.

lonely (LOHN-lee) When you feel alone.

moody (MOO-dee) When you feel sad and
    gloomy.

situation (sit-choo-AY-shun) A problem; an event
    that happens.

solve (SOLV) To find the answer to something.

Index